About This Book

2014 primary curriculum

The 2014 UK primary curriculum has statutory requirements for which spelling patterns / words should be taught in each year group.

This book meets these statutory requirements by covering the new spelling patterns and words specified for Year 3 and Year 4.

Our Year 3 books revise the graphemes covered in Year 1 and Year 2, with special attention given to the rules for adding suffixes.

Versions of the book

There are 3 versions available:
- plain text (with no words to trace over)
- cursive / joined up **WITHOUT** lead-in strokes
- cursive / joined up **WITH** lead-in strokes (not available on Amazon, only available to download from SaveTeachersSundays.com)

Accompanying resources

- passwords for over 350 Spelling games included in the book
- lesson plans, dictation sentences and other teaching resources available to purchase separately on SaveTeachersSundays.com

Contents

Contents

The sound (or) is usually represented using the letters **or** when it comes in the **middle of words**, like in the words below.

Remember: Say the word aloud, then say each letter aloud **as you write it** e.g. 'torch, t … o … r … c … h'

A **torch** is good to have in the dark.

torch   torch   _____

Lord is another name for God.

lord   lord   _____

You use a **fork** to eat with.

fork   fork   _____

In a **storm** there is strong wind and rain.

storm   storm   _____

Corn is a yellow plant that grows in fields.

corn   corn   _____

A **horn** is made of brass.

horn   horn   _____

A baby is a child that is newly **born**.

born   born   _____

A pencil gets **short** after a while.

short   short   _____

North points up on a compass face.

north   north   _____

The king rode **forth** on his horse.

forth   forth   _____

Now test yourself without looking at the words and **<u>check for yourself</u>** if you got them all right. Practice writing any words that you made mistakes on again.

The sound (or) is usually represented by the letters **ore** when it comes at the **end of words**, like in the words below.

Remember: Say the word aloud, then say each letter aloud **as you write it** e.g. 'more, m ... o ... r ... e'

Would you like **more**?

more   more   _____

The **score** in the game was 1-0.

score   score   _____

A **store** is another name for a shop.

store   store   _____

Waves from the sea crash on to the **shore**.

shore   shore   _____

Neil **tore** Gail's dress.

tore   tore   _____

Some people **snore** when they sleep.

snore   snore   _____

What do you do **before** (be/fore) you go to bed?

before   before   _____

The words below are naughty red words that belong to Nina and Neil because they use the letters oor to represent the sound (or) at the end of them.

Please shut the <u>door</u> on your way out.

door   door   _____

If someone is <u>poor</u>, they do not have much money.

poor   poor   _____

The <u>floor</u> is what you stand on when you are inside.

floor   floor   _____

Now test yourself without looking at the words and <u>check for yourself</u> if you got them all right. Practice writing any words that you made mistakes on again.

The words below are naughty red words that belong to Nina and Neil because they represent the sound (or) in unusual ways

Remember: Say the word aloud, then say each letter aloud **as you write it** e.g. 'four, f ... o ... u ... r'

The number **four** comes after the number three.

four   four   _____

If you finish **fourth** you do not get a medal.

fourth   fourth   _____

If you go on a **tour** you will see lots of things.

tour   tour   _____

A jug can be used to **pour** milk in to a bowl.

pour   pour   _____

A judge works in a **court**.

court   court   _____

When someone dies, their family will **mourn** for them.

mourn   mourn   _____

An **oar** is what you use to row a boat.

oar   oar   _____

A lion can **roar** very loudly.

roar   roar   _____

Birds can **soar** really high in the sky.

soar   soar   _____

A **board** is a flat bit of wood.

board   board   _____

Now test yourself without looking at the words and **check for yourself** if you got them all right. Practice writing any words that you made mistakes on again.

When the letter w comes before the letters or, it changes the sound that these letters represent, like in the words below.

Remember: Say the word aloud, then say each letter aloud **as you write it** e.g. 'word, w ... o ... r ... d'

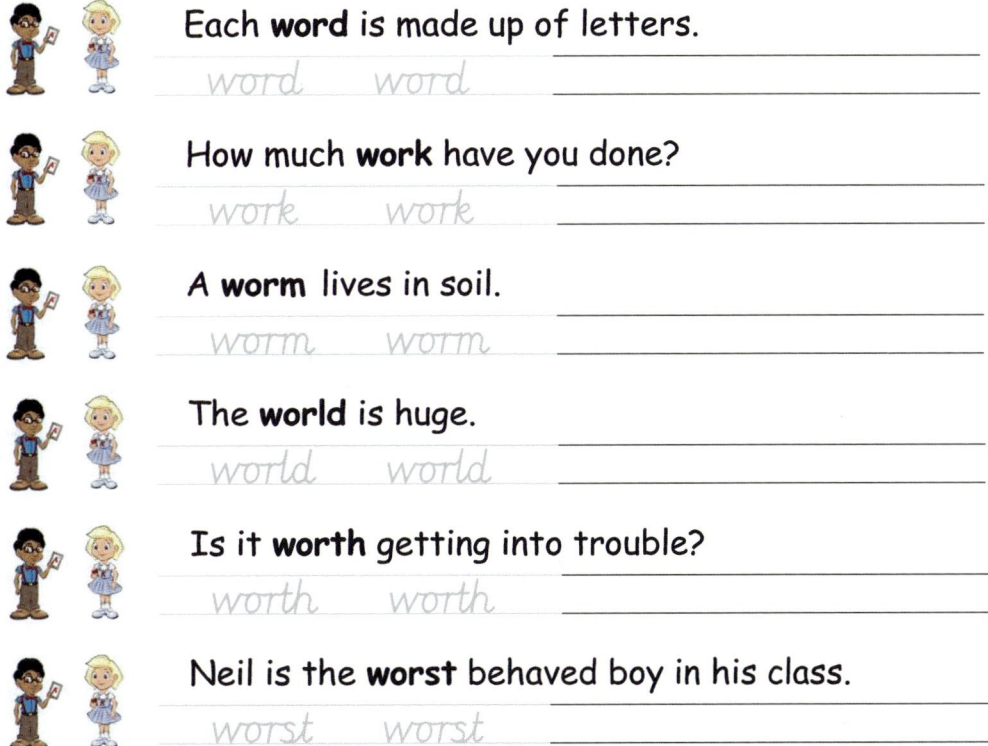

Each **word** is made up of letters.

word   word _____

How much **work** have you done?

work   work _____

A **worm** lives in soil.

worm   worm _____

The **world** is huge.

world   world _____

Is it **worth** getting into trouble?

worth   worth _____

Neil is the **worst** behaved boy in his class.

worst   worst _____

The word were is a naughty red word that belongs to Nina and Neil because it does not use the letters wor and the words sword and worn are naughty red words because they use the letters wor differently to most words with wor.

<u>Were</u> you in school on Monday?

were   were _____

Have you <u>worn</u> your new shirt?

worn   worn _____

A s<u>word</u> needs to be sharp.

sword   sword _____

Now test yourself without looking at the words and <u>**check for yourself**</u> if you got them all right. Practice writing any words that you made mistakes on again.

The sound (or) is sometimes represented by the letters aw when it comes at the end of words, like in the words below.

Remember: Say the word aloud, then say each letter aloud **as you write it** e.g. 'jaw, j ... a ... w'

Your chin and mouth are part of your **jaw.**

jaw   jaw

If something is not cooked it is **raw.**

raw   raw

A person has a hand; a dog has a **paw.**

paw   paw

Gary has never broken the **law.**

law   law

You can use a **saw** to cut wood.

saw   saw

A cat's **claw** can be very sharp.

claw   claw

In art you sometimes **draw.**

draw   draw

You can use a **straw** to drink with.

straw   straw

Beavers **gnaw** on trees with their teeth.

gnaw   gnaw

If something has a **flaw,** there is something wrong with it.

flaw   flaw

Now test yourself without looking at the words and <u>check for yourself</u> if you got them all right. Practice writing any words that you made mistakes on again.

The sound (or) is sometimes represented by the letters aw when it comes in the middle of words, like in the words below.

Remember: Say the word aloud, then say each letter aloud **as you write it** e.g. 'dawn, d ... a ... w ... n'

Dawn is when the sun first comes up.

dawn   _dawn_   _____
_____

Grass in a garden is called a **lawn.**

lawn   _lawn_   _____
_____

Bawl is another word for cry.

bawl   _bawl_   _____
_____

At first a baby can only **crawl**, not walk.

crawl   _crawl_   _____
_____

A **hawk** eats other animals.

hawk   _hawk_   _____
_____

A sea gull makes a noise called a **squawk.**

squawk   _squawk_   _____
_____

The words walk, talk and chalk are naughty red words that belong to Nina and Neil because they use the letters alk to represent the sound (ork).

You should **walk**, not run in the school.

walk   _walk_   _____
_____

Nina will always **talk**, in class.

talk   _talk_   _____
_____

Have you ever used **chalk** to draw with?

chalk   _chalk_   _____
_____

Now test yourself without looking at the words and **check for yourself** if you got them all right. Practice writing any words that you made mistakes on again.

A few words use the letters au to represent the sound (or), like in the words below.

Remember: Say the word aloud, then say each letter aloud **as you write it** e.g. 'haunt, h ... a ... u ... n ... t'

A ghost's job is to **haunt** people.

haunt   haunt _____

Wind can **cause** things to move.

cause   cause _____

If you **pause** a DVD, you stop it playing.

pause   pause _____

A rocket needs to **launch** to get to space.

launch   launch _____

Some people like **sauce** on their chips.

sauce   sauce _____

It is always Neil's **fault**.

fault   fault _____

The words below are naughty red words that belong to Nina and Neil because they use the letters au in unusual ways.

Gail works hard **because** she wants to do well.

because   because _____

Your **aunt** is your mum or dad's sister.

aunt   aunt _____

Neil **caught** the ball with only one hand!

caught   caught _____

What has your teacher **taught** you today?

taught   taught _____

Now test yourself without looking at the words and **check for yourself** if you got them all right. Practice writing any words that you made mistakes on again.

The sound (orl) is usually represented by the letters all, like in the words below.

Remember: Say the word aloud, then say each letter aloud **as you write it** e.g. 'all, a ... l ... l'

You should do your best **all** of the time.

all   _all_   _____

You can throw or kick a **ball**.

ball   _ball_   _____

Nina will **call** Gail names.

call   _call_   _____

You can get hurt if you **fall** over.

fall   _fall_   _____

You do PE in the school **hall**.

hall   _hall_   _____

Some people are short; some people are **tall**.

tall   _tall_   _____

Neil would always walk on the **wall**.

wall   _wall_   _____

Some people are **small**; some people are big.

small   _small_   _____

Do you buy your fruit from a market **stall**?

stall   _stall_   _____

The word shall is a naughty red word that belongs to Nina and Neil because it uses the letters all, but the letter a represents its short sound.

Shall we play?

shall   _shall_   _____

Now test yourself without looking at the words and **check for yourself** if you got them all right. Practice writing any words that you made mistakes on again.

The short (o) sound is represented by the letter a when it comes after the letter w or after the letters qu, like in the words below.

Remember: Say the word aloud, then say each letter aloud **as you write it** e.g. 'wasp, w ... a ... s ... p'

A **wasp** can sting you.

wasp   _wasp_   _____

A **wand** is used to do magic.

wand   _wand_   _____

Water is the best drink!

water   _water_   _____

You should **wash** your hands before you eat!

wash   _wash_   _____

If you **wander**, you walk slowly.

wander   _wander_   _____

A **swan** is white and swims on water.

swan   _swan_   _____

Neil would never **swap** toys with Gary.

swap   _swap_   _____

A **swamp** is wet and smelly.

swamp   _swamp_   _____

A team needs a **squad** of players.

squad   _squad_   _____

To make juice you **squash** the fruit.

squash   _squash_   _____

Now test yourself without looking at the words and <u>**check for yourself**</u> if you got them all right. Practice writing any words that you made mistakes on again.

The short (e) sound is usually represented by the letter e on its own. The words below are naughty red words that belong to Nina and Neil because they use the letters ea to represent the short (e) sound.

Remember: Say the word aloud, then say each letter aloud **as you write it** e.g. 'dead, d ... e ... a ... d'

If something is **dead**, it is not alive.

dead   dead _____

Your **head** is on the end of your neck.

head   head _____

How many books have you **read** this year?

read   read _____

Bread is used to make toast.

bread   bread _____

You use a knife to **spread** butter.

spread   spread _____

To have your **health** means that you are not ill.

health   health _____

Your **wealth** is about how much money you own.

wealth   wealth _____

Your **death** is when you die.

death   death _____

To calm down you can take a deep **breath**.

breath   breath _____

If someone is **deaf**, they cannot hear anything.

deaf   deaf _____

Now test yourself without looking at the words and **check for yourself** if you got them all right. Practice writing any words that you made mistakes on again.

The short (e) sound is usually represented by the letter e on its own. The words below are naughty red words that belong to Nina and Neil because they use the letters ea to represent the short (e) sound.

Remember: Say the word aloud, then say each letter aloud **as you write it** e.g. 'ready, r ... e ... a ... d ... y'

Neil will never get **ready** for bed.

ready   ready   _____

If you have **already** done something, why do it again?

already   already   _____

If something is **pleasant** then it is nice

pleasant pleasant _____

A **weapon** is something that can hurt people.

weapon   weapon   _____

The **weather** can be sunny, cloudy or rainy.

weather   weather   _____

If something is **heavy** it is hard to lift it up.

heavy   heavy   _____

What shall we do **instead**?

instead   instead   _____

Breakfast is the first meal of the day.

breakfast breakfast _____

Some people think that people go to **heaven** when they die.

heaven   heaven   _____

If you **dread** something, you are afraid of it.

dread   dread   _____

Now test yourself without looking at the words and **check for yourself** if you got them all right. Practice writing any words that you made mistakes on again.

1a) Roses can be read / red.

1b) When you have finished a book, you have read / red it.

2a) Some people feel bored / board in school.

2b) You should cut up food on a chopping bored / board.

3a) We went on a tour / tore of the castle.

3b) Mary tour / tore her dress on the bush.

4a) If you are poor / pour, you do not have much money.

4b) Will you poor / pour some water please?

5a) A judge works in a court / caught.

5b) Have you ever court / caught a fish?

6a) Have you ever warn / worn someone else's clothes?

6b) A teacher will warn / worn you if you do the wrong thing.

7a) A baby will bawl / ball if it upset.

7b) You need a bawl / ball to play some games.

Write your own sentences for these homophone pairs:

8) wonder / wander   9) fourth / forth   10) saw / sore / soar

11) bread / bred   12) sauce / source   13) morning / mourning

The sound (f) is usually represented by the letter f on its own. The words below are naughty red words that belong to Nina and Neil because they use the letters ph to represent the sound (f).

Remember: Say the word aloud, then say each letter aloud **as you write it** e.g. 'phone, p … h … o … n … e'

 Do you know your **phone** number? _____

phone   phone _____

 A **graph** is used to show some data. _____

graph   graph _____

 You can use a camera to take a **photo**. _____

photo   photo _____

 A **dolphin** will sometimes swim alongside a boat. _____

dolphin   dolphin _____

 You might get a **trophy** for winning a competition. _____

trophy   trophy _____

 A **phrase** is made up of a few words. _____

phrase   phrase _____

 A ball is the shape of a **sphere**. _____

sphere   sphere _____

 An **orphan** is a child whose parents have died. _____

orphan   orphan _____

 **Triumph** is another word for winning. _____

triumph   triumph _____

A **phobia** is a fear of something. _____

phobia   phobia _____

Now test yourself without looking at the words and **check for yourself** if you got them all right. Practice writing any words that you made mistakes on again.

The sound (w) is usually represented by the letter w on its own. The words below are naughty red words that belong to Nina and Neil because they use the letters wh to represent the sound (w).

Remember: Say the word aloud, then say each letter aloud **as you write it** e.g. 'whale, w ... h ... a ... l ... e'

A **whale** is the biggest animal in the sea.

whale   whale   _____

You turn a car by turning the **wheel**.

wheel   wheel   _____

Clouds are **white** on a sunny day.

white   white   _____

Whack is another word for hit.

whack   whack   _____

Whine is another word for moan.

whine   whine   _____

A **whiff** is a bad smell.

whiff   whiff   _____

A **wharf** is a building beside a river.

wharf   wharf   _____

If you do something on a **whim**, you do it without thinking.

whim   whim   _____

Where would you like to go on holiday?

where   where   _____

A **whisk** is used to mix things together.

whisk   whisk   _____

Now test yourself without looking at the words and **check for yourself** if you got them all right. Practice writing any words that you made mistakes on again.

The sound (shun) is most often represented by the letters tion, like in the words below.

Remember: Say the word aloud, then say each letter aloud **as you write it** e.g. 'action, a ... c ... t ... i ... o ... n'

An **action (ac/tion)** is something that you do.

action   action   _____
_____

A **question (ques/tion)** is something that you ask someone.

question   question   _____
_____

If you give someone a **direction (di/rec/tion)**, you tell them what to do.

direction   direction   _____
_____

In a **competition (com/pe/ti/tion)** you try to win.

competition   competition   _____
_____

A **collection (col/lec/tion)** is what you do when you pick something up.

collection   collection   _____
_____

If you **mention (men/tion)** something, you say it.

mention   mention   _____
_____

A helmet gives you **protection (pro/tec/tion)** from being injured.

protection   protection   _____
_____

Being polite to people will get a good **reaction (re/ac/tion)** from them.

reaction   reaction   _____
_____

In an **auction (auc/tion)** the person who bids the most wins.

auction   auction   _____
_____

If there is a **reduction (re/duc/tion)** in something, there is less of it.

reduction   reduction   _____
_____

Now test yourself without looking at the words and <u>check for yourself</u> if you got them all right. Practice writing any words that you made mistakes on again.

The sound (shun) is most often represented by the letters tion, like in the words below.

Remember: Say the word aloud, then say each letter aloud **as you write it** e.g. 'information, i ... n ... f ... o ... r ... m ... a ... t ... i ... o ... n'

You can find **information (in/for/ma/tion)** in books.

information   information   _____

A **decoration (dec/or/a/tion)** makes something look nice.

decoration   decoration   _____

A **sensation (sen/sa/tion)** is another word for a feeling.

sensation   sensation   _____

Preparation (pre/pa/ra/tion) is what you do before something.

preparation   preparation   _____

An artist might call what he makes his **creation (cre/a/tion).**

creation   creation   _____

Being lost is a bad **situation (si/tu/a/tion)** to be in.

situation   situation   _____

A **quotation (quo/ta/tion)** is something that someone said.

quotation   quotation   _____

If you feel **agitation (a/gi/ta/tion)**, you feel nervous.

agitation   agitation   _____

If you make a **donation (do/na/tion)** you give some money to charity.

donation   donation   _____

Starvation (star/va/tion) happens when there is no food to eat.

starvation   starvation   _____

Now test yourself without looking at the words and <u>check for yourself</u> if you got them all right. Practice writing any words that you made mistakes on again.

The sound (zhun) is represented by the letters sion, like in the words below.

Remember: Say the word aloud, then say each letter aloud **as you write it** e.g. 'decision, d ... e ... c ... i ... s ... i ... o ... n'

When you make a choice, you make a **decision (de/ci/sion)**.

decision   decision   _____

Division (di/vi/sion) is the inverse of multiplication.

division   division   _____

How much **television (tel/e/vi/sion)** do you watch each week?

television   television   _____

PS3 and PS4 are each a **version (ver/sion)** of the PlayStation.

version   version   _____

Your birthday is a special **occasion (oc/ca/sion)**.

occasion   occasion   _____

Non-fiction writing can end with a **conclusion (con/clu/sion)**.

conclusion   conclusion   _____

If you feel **confusion (con/fu/sion)**, you do not know what to do.

confusion   confusion   _____

If you are nervous, you might feel **tension (ten/sion)**.

tension   tension   _____

If a bomb goes off, there is an **explosion (ex/plo/sion)**.

explosion   explosion   _____

Aliens coming to Earth would be an alien **invasion (in/va/sion)**.

invasion   invasion   _____

Now test yourself without looking at the words and **<u>check for yourself</u>** if you got them all right. Practice writing any words that you made mistakes on again.

The sound (shun) is represented by the letters cian when it is used in the name of a job and is represented by the letters ssion at the end of some words.

Remember: Say the word aloud, then say each letter aloud **as you write it** e.g. 'discussion, d … i … s … c … u … s … s … i … o … n'

In a **discussion (dis/cus/sion)** you talk with other people.

discussion   discussion   _____

In school you need to get **permission (per/mis/sion)** to go to the toilet.

permission   permission   _____

The **expression (ex/pres/sion)** on your face shows how you are feeling.

expression   expression   _____

A **possession (pos/ses/sion)** is something that you own.

possession   possession   _____

A spy is given a **mission (mis/sion)** to carry out.

mission   mission   _____

A **magician (ma/gi/cian)** does magic tricks.

magician   magician   _____

A **politician (pol/i/ti/cian)** needs to win an election.

politician   politician   _____

A **musician (mu/si/cian)** plays music.

musician   musician   _____

An **electrician (e/lec/tri/cian)** needs to know about wires.

electrician   electrician   _____

An **optician (op/ti/cian)** checks people's eyesight.

optician   optician   _____

Now test yourself without looking at the words and **check for yourself** if you got them all right. Practice writing any words that you made mistakes on again.

The sound (chuh) is represented by the letters ture when it comes at the end of words, like in the words below.

Remember: Say the word aloud, then say each letter aloud **as you write it** e.g. 'picture, p … i … c … t … u … r … e'

In art you might paint a **picture (pic/ture)**.

picture   picture   _____

Tomorrow is in the **future (fu/ture)**.

future   future   _____

Animals and plants are part of **nature (na/ture)**.

nature   nature   _____

A trap can be used to **capture (cap/ture)** an animal.

capture   capture   _____

Going to the moon would be a great **adventure (ad/ven/ture)**.

adventure   adventure   _____

The **temperature (tem/per/a/ture)** is how hot or cold it is.

temperature   temperature   _____

The tables and chairs are part of the **furniture (fur/ni/ture)**.

furniture   furniture   _____

Cake **mixture (mix/ture)** needs flour, eggs, water and sugar.

mixture   mixture   _____

Creature (crea/ture) is another word for animal.

creature   creature   _____

A **vulture (vul/ture)** eats what other animals kill and leave after them.

vulture   vulture   _____

Now test yourself without looking at the words and **check for yourself** if you got them all right. Practice writing any words that you made mistakes on again.

The sound (chuh) is represented by the letters ture and the sound (shuh) is represented by the letters sure at the end of words.

Remember: Say the word aloud, then say each letter aloud **as you write it** e.g. 'texture, t ... e ... x ... t ... u ... r ... e'

The **texture (tex/ture)** of an object is how it feels e.g. rough or smooth.

texture   texture   _____

If a tyre runs over something sharp, it may **puncture (punc/ture).**

puncture   puncture   _____

In a **lecture (lec/ture)** you sit and listen to someone talk.

lecture   lecture   _____

You should sit with a straight back to have a good **posture (pos/ture).**

posture   posture   _____

The **structure (struc/ture)** of something is how it is put together.

structure   structure   _____

You can use a ruler to **measure (mea/sure)** length.

measure   measure   _____

If you enjoy something, you feel **pleasure (plea/sure)** during it.

pleasure   pleasure   _____

Pirates search for **treasure (trea/sure).**

treasure   treasure   _____

In an exam you might feel **pressure (pres/sure)** to do well.

pressure   pressure   _____

Your **leisure (lei/sure)** time is when you are not working.

leisure   leisure   _____

Now test yourself without looking at the words and **check for yourself** if you got them all right. Practice writing any words that you made mistakes on again.

The short (u) sound is represented by the letters ou in very few words.

Remember: Say the word aloud, then say each letter aloud **as you write it** e.g. 'young, y ... o ... u ... n ... g'

Children are **young** people.

young   *young*   _____
_____

Can you **touch** your toes and keep your legs straight?

touch   *touch*   _____
_____

Which **country (coun/try)** do you live in?

country   *country*   _____
_____

Your **cousin (cou/sin)** is your aunt or your uncle's child.

cousin   *cousin*   _____
_____

A **couple (cou/ple)** means two.

couple   *couple*   _____
_____

If you are brave, you have **courage (cou/rage)**.

courage   *courage*   _____
_____

If you **double (dou/ble)** a number, you multiply it by two.

double   *double*   _____
_____

Neil always gets into **trouble (trou/ble).**

trouble   *trouble*   _____
_____

A **southern (sou/thern)** wind blows from the south.

southern   *southern*   _____
_____

You eat food to **nourish (nou/rish)** your body.

nourish   *nourish*   _____
_____

Now test yourself without looking at the words and **check for yourself** if you got them all right. Practice writing any words that you made mistakes on again.

The sound (shus) is usually represented using the letters cious at the end of words, and the letters ous are used at the end of a number of words.

Remember: Say the word aloud, then say each letter aloud **as you write it** e.g. 'vicious, v ... i ... c ... i ... o ... u ... s'

A shark can be very **vicious (vi/cious)**.

vicious   _vicious_   _____

If something is **precious (pre/cious)**, then it is valuable.

precious   _precious_   _____

Delicious (del/i/cious) means very tasty.

delicious   _delicious_   _____

Tremendous (tre/men/dous) is another word for great.

tremendous   _tremendous_   _____

Enormous (e/nor/mous) means very big.

enormous   _enormous_   _____

If you are **generous (gen/er/ous)**, then you help other people.

generous   _generous_   _____

Conspicuous (con/spic/u/ous) means easy to spot or notice.

conspicuous   _conspicuous_   _____

Fabulous (fab/u/lous) is another word for brilliant.

fabulous   _fabulous_   _____

Horrendous (hor/ren/dous) is another word for awful.

horrendous   _horrendous_   _____

Being **incredulous (in/cred/u/lous)** means you don't believe something.

incredulous   _incredulous_   _____

Now test yourself without looking at the words and **check for yourself** if you got them all right. Practice writing any words that you made mistakes on again.

For the words below the suffix ous is just added to the end of them. There is no need to change the base word, except for the word marvellous, in which the final l is doubled.

Base word + Suffix	New word	1st try	2nd try	3rd try
danger + ous	dangerous	*dangerous*		
hazard + ous	hazardous	*hazardous*		
prosper + ous	prosperous	*prosperous*		
poison + ous	poisonous	*poisonous*		
joy + ous	joyous	*joyous*		
mountain + ous	mountainous	*mountainous*		
scandal + ous	scandalous	*scandalous*		
ponder + ous	ponderous	*ponderous*		
marvel + ous	marvellous	*marvellous*		

When adding the suffix ous to a base word ending in the letter y, the letter y needs to be changed to the letter i.

When adding the suffix ous to a base word ending in the letter e, drop the letter e. (If the base word ends in ce, change the letter e to the letter i).

Base word + Suffix	New word	1st try	2nd try	3rd try
vary + ous	various	various		
glory + ous	glorious	glorious		
luxury + ous	luxurious	luxurious		
envy + ous	envious	envious		
fame + ous	famous	famous		
nerve + ous	nervous	nervous		
ridicule + ous	ridiculous	ridiculous		
space + ous	spacious	spacious		
grace + ous	gracious	gracious		

The long (e) sound is usually represented by the letter i when it comes before the letters ous, although court**e**ous and hid**e**ous use the letter e instead.

Remember: Say the word aloud, then say each letter aloud **as you write it** e.g. 'serious, s … e … r … i … o … u … s'

Very **serious (ser/i/ous)** people do not laugh very much.

serious   serious   _____

What was your **previous (pre/vi/ous)** year group?

previous   previous   _____

If something is **obvious (ob/vi/ous)** it is easy to see or notice.

obvious   obvious   _____

If you are **curious (cur/i/ous)** then you always ask questions.

curious   curious   _____

Furious (fur/i/ous) means very angry.

furious   furious   _____

Tedious (te/di/ous) is another word for boring.

tedious   tedious   _____

Precarious (pre/car/i/ous) means unsafe.

precarious   precarious   _____

 Devious (dev/i/ous) means sneaky.

devious   devious   _____

Courteous (cour/te/ous) means polite.

courteous   courteous   _____

Hideous (hi/de/ous) means very ugly.

hideous   hideous   _____

Now test yourself without looking at the words and **check for yourself** if you got them all right. Practice writing any words that you made mistakes on again.

When adding the suffix ous to a base word ending in the letters our, the letters our need to change to or.

Usually when adding the suffix ous to a base word ending in the letter e, you drop the letter e, however if the word ends in ge you keep the e.

Base word + Suffix	New word	1st try	2nd try	3rd try
humour + ous	humorous	*humorous*		
vigour + ous	vigorous	*vigorous*		
rigour + ous	rigorous	*rigorous*		
glamour + ous	glamorous	*glamorous*		
odour + ous	odorous	*odorous*		
courage + ous	courageous	*courageous*		
gorge + ous	gorgeous	*gorgeous*		
outrage + ous	outrageous	*outrageous*		

For the words below the suffix ly is just added to the end of them.

There is no need to change the base word.

Base word + Suffix	New word	1st try	2nd try	3rd try
quick + ly	quickly	*quickly*	_____	_____
near + ly	nearly	*nearly*	_____	_____
close + ly	closely	*closely*	_____	_____
love + ly	lovely	*lovely*	_____	_____
bold + ly	boldly	*boldly*	_____	_____
proud + ly	proudly	*proudly*	_____	_____
slow + ly	slowly	*slowly*	_____	_____
loud + ly	loudly	*loudly*	_____	_____
soft + ly	softly	*softly*	_____	_____

All of the base words below end in l. Make sure that you have the double l when you add suffix ly to them.

Base word + Suffix	New word	1st try	2nd try	3rd try
usual + ly	usually	usually		
actual + ly	actually	actually		
eventual + ly	eventually	eventually		
final + ly	finally	finally		
normal + ly	normally	normally		
careful + ly	carefully	carefully		
initial + ly	initially	initially		
gradual + ly	gradually	gradually		
equal + ly	equally	equally		

Name: _____   Date: _____   **Change y to i**

When you add a suffix to a word that ends with the letter y, you need to change the letter y to the letter i, except when adding ing.

Base word + Suffix	New word	1st try	2nd try	3rd try
happy + ly	happily	*happily*		
lazy + ly	lazily	*lazily*		
easy + ly	easily	*easily*		
heavy + ly	heavily	*heavily*		
ready + ly	readily	*readily*		
angry + ly	angrily	*angrily*		
lucky + ly	luckily	*luckily*		
busy + ly	busily	*busily*		
noisy + ly	noisily	*noisily*		

Name: _____   Date: _____   **Suffix ly – drop e**

When you add the suffix ly to a word that ends in the letters le, you need to drop the letter e

Base word + Suffix	New word	1st try	2nd try	3rd try
gentle + ly	gently	gently	_____	_____
possible + ly	possibly	possibly	_____	_____
simple + ly	simply	simply	_____	_____
reasonable + ly	reasonably	reasonably	_____	_____
capable + ly	capably	capably	_____	_____
terrible + ly	terribly	terribly	_____	_____
sensible + ly	sensibly	sensibly	_____	_____
reliable + ly	reliably	reliably	_____	_____
horrible + ly	horribly	horribly	_____	_____

The sound (ik) is usually represented by the letters ic when it comes at the end of words of more than one syllable, like in the words below.

Remember: Say the word aloud, then say each letter aloud **as you write it** e.g. 'traffic, t ... r ... a ... f ... f ... i ... c'

If there are too many cars then there is **traffic (traf/fic)**.

traffic   traffic _____

If something is **basic (ba/sic)** then it is easy to do.

basic   basic _____

A chair can be made from **plastic (plas/tic)**.

plastic   plastic _____

What **topic (top/ic)** are you learning about in science?

topic   topic _____

If you are very worried, you might **panic (pan/ic)**.

panic   panic _____

The lights in your school are **electric (e/lec/tric)**.

electric   electric _____

A **comic (com/ic)** is a book that tells a story and uses pictures.

comic   comic _____

A **picnic (pic/nic)** is when you sit and eat on the ground.

picnic   picnic _____

An **attic (at/tic)** is the part of a house just under the roof.

attic   attic _____

If something is **tragic (tra/gic)**, then it is very sad.

tragic   tragic _____

Now test yourself without looking at the words and **check for yourself** if you got them all right. Practice writing any words that you made mistakes on again.

Name: _____ Date: _____ **Suffix ly – add ally**

When a word ends in the letters ic, you need to add the letters ally, not just ly (except for the word publicly)

Base word + Suffix	New word	1st try	2nd try	3rd try
basic + ly	basically	*basically*		
specific + ly	specifically	*specifically*		
magic + ly	magically	*magically*		
frantic + ly	frantically	*frantically*		
dramatic + ly	dramatically	*dramatically*		
comic + ly	comically	*comically*		
tragic + ly	tragically	*tragically*		
music + ly	musically	*musically*		
public + ly	publicly	*publicly*		

Name: _____ Date: _____ **Suffix en**

For each word see if the suffix rule is 'just add', 'double the final consonant' or 'drop the e'

Base word + Suffix	New word	1st try	2nd try	3rd try
fright + en	frighten	*frighten*		
soften + en	soften	*soften*		
fast + en	fasten	*fasten*		
rot + en	rotten	*rotten*		
hid + en	hidden	*hidden*		
red + en	redden	*redden*		
take + en	taken	*taken*		
spoke + en	spoken	*spoken*		
haste + en	hasten	*hasten*		

Name: _____   Date: _____   **Suffix ity**

Suffix ity is a vowel suffix, so when you add it to words ending in e you need to drop the e

Base word + Suffix	New word	1st try	2nd try	3rd try
minor + ity	minority	minority		
complex + ity	complexity	complexity		
electric + ity	electricity	electricity		
equal + ity	equality	equality		
universe + ity	university	university		
active + ity	activity	activity		
secure + ity	security	security		
dense + ity	density	density		
continue + ity	continuity	continuity		

Name: _____   Date: _____   Prefix dis

A prefix is added to the front of a word. The prefix dis has a negative meaning e.g. disorder means not in order

Prefix + Base word	New word	1st try	2nd try	3rd try
dis + agree	disagree	*disagree*		
dis + appear	disappear	*disappear*		
dis + obey	disobey	*disobey*		
dis + trust	distrust	*distrust*		
dis + grace	disgrace	*disgrace*		
dis + order	disorder	*disorder*		
dis + able	disable	*disable*		
dis + like	dislike	*dislike*		
dis + comfort	discomfort	*discomfort*		

Name: _____   Date: _____   **Prefix mis**

A prefix is added to the front of a word. The prefix mis has a negative meaning e.g. misuse means to use in the wrong way

Prefix + Base word	New word	1st try	2nd try	3rd try
mis + lead	mislead	*mislead*		
mis + use	misuse	*misuse*		
mis + trust	mistrust	*mistrust*		
mis + fortune	misfortune	*misfortune*		
mis + match	mismatch	*mismatch*		
mis + place	misplace	*misplace*		
mis + behave	misbehave	*misbehave*		
mis + fit	misfit	*misfit*		
mis + judge	misjudge	*misjudge*		

The prefix un has a negative meaning e.g. unable means not able. The prefix in can have a negative meaning or can mean put into e.g. inhale means to breathe in air

Prefix + Base word	New word	1ˢᵗ try	2ⁿᵈ try	3ʳᵈ try
in + correct	incorrect	incorrect		
in + active	inactive	inactive		
in + complete	incomplete	incomplete		
in + secure	insecure	insecure		
in + come	income	income		
in + hale	inhale	inhale		
in + put	input	input		
un + able	unable	unable		
un + even	uneven	uneven		

The prefix im can have a negative meaning e.g. immature means not mature or it can mean into e.g. imprison means put in prison

Prefix + Base word	New word	1st try	2nd try	3rd try
im + possible	impossible	impossible		
im + practical	impractical	impractical		
im + mature	immature	immature		
im + moral	immoral	immoral		
im + perfect	imperfect	imperfect		
im + pact	impact	impact		
im + port	import	import		
im + prison	imprison	imprison		
im + migrant	immigrant	immigrant		

The prefixes il and ir have negative meanings e.g. illegal means not legal and irregular means not regular

Prefix + Base word	New word	1st try	2nd try	3rd try
il + legal	illegal	illegal		
il + legible	illegible	illegible		
il + logical	illogical	illogical		
il + legitimate	illegitimate	illegitmate		
ir + regular	irregular	irregular		
ir + relevant	irrelevant	irrelevant		
ir + resistible	irresistible	irresistible		
ir + reversible	irreversible	irreversible		
ir + responsible	irresponsible	irresponsible		

39

The prefix re means to do again e.g. recycle means to use again and the prefix sub means under e.g. subway means underground

Prefix + Base word	New word	1st try	2nd try	3rd try
re + visit	revisit	*revisit*	_____	_____
re + phrase	rephrase	*rephrase*	_____	_____
re + cycle	recycle	*recycle*	_____	_____
re + write	rewrite	*rewrite*	_____	_____
sub + merge	submerge	*submerge*	_____	_____
sub + marine	submarine	*submarine*	_____	_____
sub + title	subtitle	*subtitle*	_____	_____
sub + heading	subheading	*subheading*	_____	_____
sub + way	subway	*subway*	_____	_____

The short (u) sound is sometimes represented by the letter o, like in the words below.

Remember: Say the word aloud, then say each letter aloud **as you write it** e.g. 'wonder, w … o … n … d … e … r'

If you **wonder (won/der)** about something, you think about it.

wonder _____ _wonder_ _____ _____

Parents **worry (wor/ry)** about their children.

worry _____ _worry_ _____ _____

A tent will **cover (co/ver)** you when you go camping.

cover _____ _cover_ _____ _____

You bake things in an **oven (o/ven)**.

oven _____ _oven_ _____ _____

A **dove** is a bird that is often white.

dove _____ _dove_ _____ _____

Zero is the same as **nothing (no/thing)**.

nothing _____ _nothing_ _____ _____

An **onion (on/ion)** can make your eyes water when you cut it.

onion _____ _onion_ _____ _____

Your mum is a **woman (wo/man)**.

woman _____ _woman_ _____ _____

Your friends should **comfort (com/fort)** you when you're upset.

comfort _____ _comfort_ _____ _____

You can use a **shovel (sho/vel)** to dig a hole.

shovel _____ _shovel_ _____ _____

Now test yourself without looking at the words and **check for yourself** if you got them all right. Practice writing any words that you made mistakes on again.

The sounds (bul) and (dul) are nearly always represented by the letters ble or the letters dle when they come at the end of words.

Remember: Say the word aloud, then say each letter aloud **as you write it** e.g. 'pebble, p ... e ... b ... b ... l ... e'

A **pebble (peb/ble)** is a small, round stone.

pebble   _pebble_   _____
_____

A **bubble (bub/ble)** will burst if you touch it.

bubble   _bubble_   _____
_____

If you **treble (tre/ble)** a number, you multiply it by three.

treble   _treble_   _____
_____

Marble (mar/ble) is a hard, shiny material.

marble   _marble_   _____
_____

The **bible (bi/ble)** is a holy book for Christians.

bible   _bible_   _____
_____

To open a door, you turn the **handle (han/dle)**.

handle   _handle_   _____
_____

You use a **needle (nee/dle)** and thread to sow.

needle   _needle_   _____
_____

A dog will **paddle (pad/dle)** to swim in the water.

paddle   _paddle_   _____
_____

A **puddle (pud/dle)** is made by the rain.

puddle   _puddle_   _____
_____

When you ride a horse, you sit in a **saddle (sad/dle)**.

saddle   _saddle_   _____
_____

Now test yourself without looking at the words and <u>check for yourself</u> if you got them all right. Practice writing any words that you made mistakes on again.

The sound (tul) is nearly always represented by the letters tle and the sound (kul) is most often represented by the letters kle at the end of words.

Remember: Say the word aloud, then say each letter aloud **as you write it** e.g. 'rattle, r ... a ... t ... t ... l ... e'

A **rattle (rat/tle)** is a toy for a baby that makes noise.

rattle   rattle   _____

Little (lit/tle) means small.

little   little   _____

Do you bring a **bottle (bot/tle)** of water to school?

bottle   bottle   _____

A **beetle (bee/tle)** is an insect with a hard shell and pincers.

beetle   beetle   _____

A **turtle (tur/tle)** is an animal that swims and has a hard shell.

turtle   turtle   _____

Your **ankle (an/kle)** is above your foot.

ankle   ankle   _____

If you **tickle (tic/kle)**, someone you make them laugh.

tickle   tickle   _____

A jewel will **sparkle (spar/kle)** in the light.

sparkle   sparkle   _____

If you **chuckle (chuc/kle)**, you have a little laugh.

chuckle   chuckle   _____

When the other team have the ball, you try to **tackle (tac/kle)** them.

tackle   tackle   _____

Now test yourself without looking at the words and **check for yourself** if you got them all right. Practice writing any words that you made mistakes on again.

The sound (ful) is represented by the letters fle (unless it is suffix ful) and the sound (gul) is nearly always represented by the letters gle at the end of words.

Remember: Say the word aloud, then say each letter aloud **as you write it** e.g. 'rifle, r ... i ... f ... l ... e'

A **rifle (ri/fle)** is a gun with a long barrel.

rifle   *rifle*   _____

A **trifle (tri/fle)** is a desert with different layers.

trifle   *trifle*   _____

A **waffle (waf/fle)** is made from potato and is the shape of a grid.

waffle   *waffle*   _____

If you **baffle (baf/fle)** someone, you confuse them.

baffle   *baffle*   _____

A **triangle (tri/an/gle)** is a 2-D shape with 3 sides.

triangle   *triangle*   _____

How many balls can you **juggle (jug/gle)** at the same time?

juggle   *juggle*   _____

If you **giggle (gig/gle)**, you laugh at something silly.

giggle   *giggle*   _____

The **jungle (jun/gle)** has lots of big trees and wild animals.

jungle   *jungle*   _____

An **eagle (ea/gle)** eats other small birds or animals.

eagle   *eagle*   _____

Burgle (bur/gle) means steal.

burgle   *burgle*   _____

Now test yourself without looking at the words and **check for yourself** if you got them all right. Practice writing any words that you made mistakes on again.

The sounds (pul), (sul) and (zul) are usually represented by the letters ple, stle and zle at the end of words. The cle spelling is rarely used for the sound (kul).

Remember: Say the word aloud, then say each letter aloud **as you write it** e.g. 'staple, s … t … a … p … l … e'

A **staple (sta/ple)** is used to attach pages of paper together.

staple   staple   _____

_____

If you **triple (tri/ple)** a number, then you multiply it by 3.

triple   triple   _____

_____

If you **topple (top/ple)** something, you knock it over.

topple   topple   _____

_____

If you drop a stone in a pool of water, the water will **ripple (rip/ple)**.

ripple   ripple   _____

_____

A king lives in a **castle (cas/stle)**.

castle   castle   _____

_____

A referee will blow his **whistle (whi/stle)** to stop a game.

whistle   whistle   _____

_____

A car is a type of **vehicle (ve/hi/cle)**.

vehicle   vehicle   _____

_____

Your **uncle (un/cle)** is your mum or your dad's brother.

uncle   uncle   _____

_____

A jigsaw **puzzle (puz/zle)** has pieces that need to be put together.

puzzle   puzzle   _____

_____

A **muzzle (muz/zle)** goes around a dog's mouth to stop it biting people.

muzzle   muzzle   _____

_____

Now test yourself without looking at the words and <u>check for yourself</u> if you got them all right. Practice writing any words that you made mistakes on again.

The sound (ul) is represented by the letters el at the end of some words, like in the words below.

Remember: Say the word aloud, then say each letter aloud **as you write it** e.g. 'model, m ... o ... d ... e ... l'

A **model (mo/del)** has her photo taken a lot.

model   model _____

_____

How far do you have to **travel (tra/vel)** to school?

travel   travel _____

_____

You should **label (lab/el)** your uniform with your name.

label   label _____

_____

A **tunnel (tun/nel)** runs under the ground and people travel through it.

tunnel   tunnel _____

_____

If someone is **cruel (cru/el)**, they are not very nice.

cruel   cruel _____

_____

A **barrel (bar/rel)** is a larger container for liquid.

barrel   barrel _____

_____

You use a **towel (tow/el)** to dry yourself.

towel   towel _____

_____

A **jewel (jew/el)** sparkles and is worth a lot of money.

jewel   jewel _____

_____

A **camel (cam/el)** is an animal with one or two humps on its back.

camel   camel _____

_____

What **level (lev/el)** does your teacher like the noise to be at?

level   level _____

_____

Now test yourself without looking at the words and **check for yourself** if you got them all right. Practice writing any words that you made mistakes on again.

The sound (ul) is represented by the letters al at the end of some words, like in the words below.

Remember: Say the word aloud, then say each letter aloud **as you write it** e.g. 'coral, c ... o ... r ... a ... l'

Coral (cor/al) is made up of colourful plants that live in the water.

coral   coral   _____

_____

An **oval (o/val)** is like a squashed circle.

oval   oval   _____

_____

You **dial (di/al)** 999 if you need the police.

dial   dial   _____

_____

If two things are **equal (e/qual)** then they are the same.

equal   equal   _____

_____

You might get a gold **medal (med/al)** if you win a race.

medal   medal   _____

_____

Metal (met/al) is used to make pots and pans.

metal   metal   _____

_____

Each **petal (pet/al)** on a flower is brightly coloured to attract insects.

petal   petal   _____

_____

A king and a queen are **royal (roy/al)** people.

royal   royal   _____

_____

To get the **total (to/tal)** of two numbers you add them up.

total   total   _____

_____

You should be **loyal (loy/al)** to your friends.

loyal   loyal   _____

_____

Now test yourself without looking at the words and **check for yourself** if you got them all right. Practice writing any words that you made mistakes on again.

The sound (il) is nearly always represented by the letters il at the end of words of more than one syllable and a very few words begin with the letters gn.

Remember: Say the word aloud, then say each letter aloud **as you write it** e.g. 'pupil, p ... u ... p ... i ... l'

A **pupil (pup/il)** is a child who is in a school.

pupil　　*pupil*　　_____

A witch is supposed to be **evil (e/vil)**.

evil　　*evil*　　_____

Do you write with a pen or a **pencil (pen/cil)**?

pencil　　*pencil*　　_____

A **fossil (fos/sil)** is an animal that has been dead for a very long time.

fossil　　*fossil*　　_____

You have a left and a right **nostril (nos/tril)** in your nose.

nostril　　*nostril*　　_____

A **council (coun/cil)** is a group of people who run something.

council　　*council*　　_____

A **gnome** is a short statue that some people have in their garden.

gnome　　*gnome*　　_____

A beaver uses his teeth to **gnaw** on a tree.

gnaw　　*gnaw*　　_____

A **gnat** is a small fly.

gnat　　*gnat*　　_____

A **gnarled (gnarl/ed)** tree is old and twisted.

gnarled　　*gnarled*　　_____

Now test yourself without looking at the words and **check for yourself** if you got them all right. Practice writing any words that you made mistakes on again.

The words below are some of the few words that begin with the letters kn.

Remember: Say the word aloud, then say each letter aloud **as you write it** e.g. 'knock, k ... n ... o ... c ... k'

You **knock** on a door to let someone know that you are outside it.

knock   _knock_   _____

Your **knee** is halfway down your leg

knee   _knee_   _____

You turn the **knob** on a door to open it.

knob   _knob_   _____

You tie a **knot** in your shoe laces to keep your shoes on.

knot   _knot_   _____

If you **knit**, you use needles and wool to make clothes.

knit   _knit_   _____

A **knight** wears armour and fights for the king or queen.

knight   _knight_   _____

You use a fork and a **knife** to eat.

knife   _knife_   _____

People **kneel** to pray when they go to church.

kneel   _kneel_   _____

You have a **knuckle (knuc/kle)** at the bottom of each finger.

knuckle   _knuckle_   _____

You use your hands to **knead** dough before you bake it.

knead   _knead_   _____

Now test yourself without looking at the words and **check for yourself** if you got them all right. Practice writing any words that you made mistakes on again.

The words below are some of the few words that begin with the letters wr.

Remember: Say the word aloud, then say each letter aloud **as you write it** e.g. 'write, w ... r ... i ... t ... e'

Do you **write** with your left or your right hand?

write   _write_   _____

Teachers put a cross next to **wrong** answers.

wrong   _wrong_   _____

You **wrap** a Christmas present before you give it away.

wrap   _wrap_   _____

Your **wrist** is at the bottom of your hand.

wrist   _wrist_   _____

You use a **wrench** to tighten a bolt.

wrench   _wrench_   _____

A **wreath** is a circle of flowers.

wreath   _wreath_   _____

A worm will **wriggle (wrig/gle)** to move.

wriggle   _wriggle_   _____

A **wrinkle (wrin/kle)** is a crease in your skin.

wrinkle   _wrinkle_   _____

If you **wrestle (wre/stle)** someone, you try to push them around.

wrestle   _wrestle_   _____

A **wry** smile is a little smile that you might give when you realise something.

wry   _wry_   _____

Now test yourself without looking at the words and <u>**check for yourself**</u> if you got them all right. Practice writing any words that you made mistakes on again.

The sound (s) is often represented by the letters ce when it comes at the end of words, like in the words below.

Remember: Say the word aloud, then say each letter aloud **as you write it** e.g. 'mice, m ... i ... c ... e'

Mice are animals that live in holes and like cheese.

mice   *mice* _____

Rice is a type of food that is small and can be brown, white or yellow.

rice   *rice* _____

In a **race** you try to go faster than everyone else.

race   *race* _____

The stars and the moon are in **space**.

space   *space* _____

Your eyes and nose are on your **face**.

face   *face* _____

Do you like tomato **sauce** on your chips?

sauce   *sauce* _____

You have to go to school - you have no **choice** about it.

choice   *choice* _____

A **fence** goes around a field to stop animals getting in or out.

fence   *fence* _____

Do you like to **dance** when you hear music?

dance   *dance* _____

Can you **bounce** a ball with your weak hand?

bounce   *bounce* _____

Now test yourself without looking at the words and <u>check for yourself</u> if you got them all right. Practice writing any words that you made mistakes on again.

The sound (s) is sometimes represented by the letters se when it comes at the end of words, like in the words below.

Remember: Say the word aloud, then say each letter aloud **as you write it** e.g. 'case, c ... a ... s ... e'

You put your things in a **case** when you go on holiday.

case   case   _____

_____

A pyramid is named after the shape of its **base**.

base   base   _____

_____

In a **chase** you try to catch someone.

chase   chase   _____

_____

A balloon will **rise** into the air.

rise   rise   _____

_____

If someone is **wise**, then they make good choices.

wise   wise   _____

_____

If you jump out at someone you can **surprise (sur/prise)** them.

surprise   surprise   _____

_____

A **rose** is a type of flower.

rose   rose   _____

_____

You should always **close** doors after you go through them.

close   close   _____

_____

If you do not know a language, it makes no **sense** when you hear it.

sense   sense   _____

_____

Can you hear any **noise**?

noise   noise   _____

_____

Now test yourself without looking at the words and **check for yourself** if you got them all right. Practice writing any words that you made mistakes on again.

The sound (s) is sometimes represented by the letter c when it comes before the letters e, i or y, like in the words below.

Remember: Say the word aloud, then say each letter aloud **as you write it** e.g. 'centre, c … e … n … t … r … e'

Centre (cen/tre) is another word for middle.

centre   centre   _____

An **accident (ac/ci/dent)** is something bad that was not meant to happen.

accident   accident   _____

A **century (cen/tur/y)** is 100 years.

century   century   _____

Certain (cer/tain) means sure.

certain   certain   _____

A **circle (cir/cle)** is a round 2-D shape.

circle   circle   _____

Decide (de/cide) is another word for choose.

decide   decide   _____

Running and cycling are types of **exercise (ex/er/cise)**.

exercise   exercise   _____

If you are ill, you might take some **medicine (med/i/cine)**.

medicine   medicine   _____

If something is **recent (re/cent)**, then it happened not very long ago.

recent   recent   _____

Which people are **special (spe/cial)** to you?

special   special   _____

Now test yourself without looking at the words and **check for yourself** if you got them all right. Practice writing any words that you made mistakes on again.

The sound (j) is always represented by the letters **ge** when it comes **after a long vowel sound** or after the letters n or r.

Remember: Say the word aloud, then say each letter aloud **as you write it** e.g. 'cage, c ... a ... g ... e'

Animals are kept in a **cage** at the zoo.

cage   _cage_   _____

If you feel **rage**, then you are very angry.

rage   _rage_   _____

You perform a play on a **stage**.

stage   _stage_   _____

If you have an **urge** to do something, you want to do it.

urge   _urge_   _____

A **hinge** lets a door swing open and shut.

hinge   _hinge_   _____

Large is another word for big.

large   _large_   _____

Would you like an apple or an **orange (or/ange)**?

orange   _orange_   _____

How long do you take to **change** for PE?

change   _change_   _____

You can use a **sponge** to wash yourself in the bath.

sponge   _sponge_   _____

If you **oblige (o/blige)** someone, you do something for them.

oblige   _oblige_   _____

Now test yourself without looking at the words and **check for yourself** if you got them all right. Practice writing any words that you made mistakes on again.

The sound (j) is always represented by the letters **dge** when it comes **after a short vowel sound**, like in the words below.

Remember: Say the word aloud, then say each letter aloud **as you write it** e.g. 'edge, e ... d ... g ... e'

A sphere does not have an **edge**.

edge   *edge*   _ _ _ _ _ _ _ _ _ _ _ _ _ _ _ _ _ _

A **hedge** is a bush that people trim and cut.

hedge   *hedge*   _ _ _ _ _ _ _ _ _ _ _ _ _ _ _ _ _ _

You can slide down a hill in a **sledge** when it snows.

sledge   *sledge*   _ _ _ _ _ _ _ _ _ _ _ _ _ _ _ _ _ _

For your birthday you might wear a **badge** that shows your age.

badge   *badge*   _ _ _ _ _ _ _ _ _ _ _ _ _ _ _ _ _ _

If you **dodge** something, you get out of the way of it.

dodge   *dodge*   _ _ _ _ _ _ _ _ _ _ _ _ _ _ _ _ _ _

Fudge is a type of chocolate.

fudge   *fudge*   _ _ _ _ _ _ _ _ _ _ _ _ _ _ _ _ _ _

A **judge** is in charge of a court.

judge   *judge*   _ _ _ _ _ _ _ _ _ _ _ _ _ _ _ _ _ _

If you **nudge** someone, you give them a little push.

nudge   *nudge*   _ _ _ _ _ _ _ _ _ _ _ _ _ _ _ _ _ _

A **bridge** can let you cross over a river.

bridge   *bridge*   _ _ _ _ _ _ _ _ _ _ _ _ _ _ _ _ _ _

You put things in a **fridge** to keep them cool.

fridge   *fridge*   _ _ _ _ _ _ _ _ _ _ _ _ _ _ _ _ _ _

Now test yourself without looking at the words and **check for yourself** if you got them all right. Practice writing any words that you made mistakes on again.

The letter g nearly always represents the sound (j) when it comes before the letters e, i or y, like in the words below.

Remember: Say the word aloud, then say each letter aloud **as you write it** e.g. 'gem, g ... e ... m'

A **gem** is another name for a jewel.

gem _gem_ _____

Some people put **gel** in their hair so that they can style it.

gel _gel_ _____

A **gerbil (ger/bil)** is a small animal, a bit like a mouse.

gerbil _gerbil_ _____

An **angel (an/gel)** has wings and a halo around its head.

angel _angel_ _____

Ginger (gin/ger) is a type of spice.

ginger _ginger_ _____

Magic (ma/gic) tricks make you wonder how they were done.

magic _magic_ _____

If something is **fragile (fra/gile)**, then it is easy to break.

fragile _fragile_ _____

A **giant (gi/ant)** is a very big person.

giant _giant_ _____

If someone is **gentle (gen/tle)**, they are careful not to hurt you.

gentle _gentle_ _____

A **giraffe (gi/raffe)** is a yellow and brown animal with a long neck.

giraffe _giraffe_ _____

Now test yourself without looking at the words and <u>**check for yourself**</u> if you got them all right. Practice writing any words that you made mistakes on again.

Quite a few words use the letter y to represent the short (i) sound, like in the words below.

Remember: Say the word aloud, then say each letter aloud **as you write it** e.g. 'gym, g ... y ... m'

Some people go to the **gym** to exercise.

gym   _gym_   _____

A **crypt** is a place that things are buried in.

crypt   _crypt_   _____

A **crystal** (crys/tal) is shiny and reflects light.

crystal   _crystal_   _____

A **gypsy** (gyp/sy) is someone who often moves where he or she lives.

gypsy   _gypsy_   _____

A **mystic** (mys/tic) is someone who thinks he or she can tell the future.

mystic   _mystic_   _____

A **mystery** (mys/ter/y) is something that cannot be understood.

mystery   _mystery_   _____

A **symbol** (sym/bol) is a sign that means something, like a dove meaning peace.

symbol   _symbol_   _____

If something is **abysmal** (a/bys/mal), it is really bad.

abysmal   _abysmal_   _____

Hypnosis (hyp/no/sis) is when someone hypnotises you.

hypnosis   _hypnosis_   _____

We breathe in **oxygen** (ox/y/gen).

oxygen   _oxygen_   _____

Now test yourself without looking at the words and **check for yourself** if you got them all right. Practice writing any words that you made mistakes on again.

Quite a few words use the letter y to represent the short (i) sound, like in the words below.

Remember: Say the word aloud, then say each letter aloud **as you write it** e.g. 'hymn, h ... y ... m ... n'

A **hymn** is a song that people sing in church.

hymn   hymn   _____

A **myth** is an old story that normally isn't true.

myth   myth   _____

A **system (sys/tem)** is a way of doing things.

system   system   _____

If an activity is **physical (phy/si/cal),** you need to use your body to do it.

physical   physical   _____

Showers are **typical (typ/i/cal)** April weather.

typical   typical   _____

The words in a song are called **lyrics (ly/rics)**.

lyrics   lyrics   _____

A **polygon (pol/y/gon)** is a 2-D shape with no gaps and straight sides.

polygon   polygon   _____

Do you wear **pyjamas (py/ja/mas)** when you go to bed?

pyjamas   pyjamas   _____

A **pyramid (py/ra/mid)** is a 3-D shape that is named by the shape of its base.

pyramid   pyramid   _____

A runny nose is a **symptom (symp/tom)** of having a cold.

symptom   symptom   _____

Now test yourself without looking at the words and **check for yourself** if you got them all right. Practice writing any words that you made mistakes on again.

Quite a few words use the letter y to represent the short (i) sound, like in the words below.

Remember: Say the word aloud, then say each letter aloud **as you write it** e.g. 'cryptic, c ... r ... y ... p ... t ... i ... c'

A **cryptic (cryp/tic)** clue is often tricky to work out the answer to.

cryptic   cryptic   _____

A **cynic (cyn/ic)** is someone who is not easily convinced.

cynic   cynic   _____

Do you know how to ride a **bicycle (bi/cy/cle)**?

bicycle   bicycle   _____

Physics (phy/sics) is the part of science that looks at forces and energy.

physics   physics   _____

Your **analysis (a/nal/y/sis)** of something is what you think about it.

analysis   analysis   _____

If you are **anonymous (a/non/y/mous)**, people do not know your name.

anonymous   anonymous   _____

If someone is **hysterical (hy/ster/i/cal)** they cannot stop laughing or crying.

hysterical   hysterical   _____

Mysterious (my/ster/i/ous) means strange and unusual.

mysterious   mysterious   _____

A square has four lines of **symmetry (sym/me/try)**.

symmetry   symmetry   _____

Can you hear the **rhythm (rhy/thm)** of a song?

rhythm   rhythm   _____

Now test yourself without looking at the words and **check for yourself** if you got them all right. Practice writing any words that you made mistakes on again.

Quite a few words use the letters ch to represent the sound (k), like in the words below.

Remember: Say the word aloud, then say each letter aloud **as you write it** e.g. 'echo, e ... c ... h ... o'

An **echo (e/cho)** is what you hear when your voice bounces back to you.

echo   echo   _____

An **ache** is a dull pain.

ache   ache   _____

Can you play a **chord** on the guitar?

chord   chord   _____

A **scheme** can be another name for a plan.

scheme   scheme   _____

What is the name of your **school**?

school   school   _____

A boat puts down an **anchor (an/chor)** so that it won't move.

anchor   anchor   _____

An **orchid (or/chid)** is a type of flower.

orchid   orchid   _____

A **chemist (chem/ist)** gives people medicine.

chemist   chemist   _____

Food goes into your **stomach (stom/ach)** when you eat it.

stomach   stomach   _____

If there were no rules there would be **chaos (cha/os)**.

chaos   chaos   _____

Now test yourself without looking at the words and **check for yourself** if you got them all right. Practice writing any words that you made mistakes on again.

Quite a few words use the letters ch to represent the sound (k), like in the words below.

Remember: Say the word aloud, then say each letter aloud **as you write it** e.g. 'architect, a ... r ... c ... h ... i ... t ... e ... c ... t'

An **architect (ar/chi/tect)** draws buildings.

architect   architect   _____

A **character (char/ac/ter)** is someone in a story.

character   character   _____

A **chorus (chor/us)** is the part of a song that is repeated.

chorus   chorus   _____

A priest will **christen (chri/sten)** a baby with water.

christen   christen   _____

A **mechanic (me/cha/nic)** fixes cars.

mechanic   mechanic   _____

An **orchestra (or/che/stra)** has lots of people playing instruments.

orchestra   orchestra   _____

If something is **technical (tech/ni/cal)**, it can be hard to understand.

technical   technical   _____

A **chemical (chem/i/cal)** can be toxic to people.

chemical   chemical   _____

You need to have a good **technique (tech/nique)** to play golf.

technique   technique   _____

A **chasm** is a massive hole.

chasm   chasm   _____

Now test yourself without looking at the words and **check for yourself** if you got them all right. Practice writing any words that you made mistakes on again.

A few words use the letters sc to represent the sound (s), like in the words below.

Remember: Say the word aloud, then say each letter aloud **as you write it** e.g. 'science, s ... c ... i ... e ... n ... c ... e'

Science (sci/ence) is a subject that you do at school.

science   _science_   _____

A **scene** is one part of a film or play.

scene   _scene_   _____

A **scent** is the name for the smell from a flower.

scent   _scent_   _____

If you exercise a **muscle (mu/scle)** it will get stronger.

muscle   _muscle_   _____

A magic trick can **fascinate (fa/sci/nate)** you.

fascinate   _fascinate_   _____

Seeing your team score can **scintillate (scin/til/ate)** you.

scintillate   _scintillate_   _____

A **schedule (sche/dule)** tells you what time events will happen.

schedule   _schedule_   _____

A **scissors (scis/sors)** is used to cut things.

scissors   _scissors_   _____

A **crescent (cre/scent)** is the shape of the moon when it is not full.

crescent   _crescent_   _____

You need to have **discipline (di/sci/pline)** to train hard for something.

discipline   _discipline_   _____

Now test yourself without looking at the words and <u>**check for yourself**</u> if you got them all right. Practice writing any words that you made mistakes on again.

A very few words use the letters gue to represent the sound (g) or the letters que to represent the sound (k), like in the words below.

Remember: Say the word aloud, then say each letter aloud **as you write it** e.g. 'league, l ... e ... a ... g ... u ... e'

In a **league** a team plays all of the other teams in the **league**.

league   *league*   _____

A **rogue** is someone who is always up to mischief.

rogue   *rogue*   _____

Your **tongue** is in your mouth.

tongue   *tongue*   _____

If you are **vague** about something, you are not sure about it.

vague   *vague*   _____

Dialogue (di/a/logue) is what people say.

dialogue   *dialogue*   _____

You can write a **cheque** to pay for something.

cheque   *cheque*   _____

A **mosque** is where Muslims go to pray.

mosque   *mosque*   _____

An **antique (an/tique)** is a very old object.

antique   *antique*   _____

If something is **unique (u/nique)** it is a one-off with no copies.

unique   *unique*   _____

Plaque builds up on your teeth if you do not wash them.

plaque   *plaque*   _____

Now test yourself without looking at the words and **check for yourself** if you got them all right. Practice writing any words that you made mistakes on again.

When you add a suffix to a word ending in the letter y, you need to change the letter i to the letter y, unless you are adding suffix ing

Base word + Suffix	New word	1st try	2nd try	3rd try
carry + ing	carrying	carrying		
bury + ed	buried	buried		
funny + er	funnier	funnier		
busy + est	busiest	busiest		
merry + ment	merriment	merriment		
beauty + ful	beautiful	beautiful		
plenty + ful	plentiful	plentiful		
lazy + ness	laziness	laziness		
mercy + less	merciless	merciless		

Name: _____   Date: _____   **Change y to i and add es**

When you add suffix s to a word ending in the letter y, you need to change the letter i to the letter y and add the letters es

Base word + Suffix	New word	1st try	2nd try	3rd try
cry + s	cries	cries	_____	_____
dry + s	dries	dries	_____	_____
baby + s	babies	babies	_____	_____
army + s	armies	armies	_____	_____
berry + s	berries	berries	_____	_____
city + s	cities	cities	_____	_____
pony + s	ponies	ponies	_____	_____
lady + s	ladies	ladies	_____	_____
lorry + s	lorries	lorries	_____	_____

When you add a **vowel suffix** to a word that ends with a short vowel followed by a consonant, you need to double the final consonant

Base word + Suffix	New word	1st try	2nd try	3rd try
rub + ing	rubbing	rubbing		
dig + ing	digging	digging		
fit + ed	fitted	fitted		
spot + ed	spotted	spotted		
run + er	runner	runner		
rob + er	robber	robber		
fat + est	fattest	fattest		
sun + y	sunny	sunny		
slop + y	sloppy	sloppy		

The schwa sound is a neutral vowel sound that can be represented in many different ways. The words below use the letters ar or er to represent it.

Remember: Say the word aloud, then say each letter aloud **as you write it** e.g. 'calendar, c ... a ... l ... e ... n ... d ... a ... r'

You use a **calendar (ca/len/dar)** to see what date it is.

calendar   calendar   _____

Grammar (gram/mar) is about the rules for writing correctly.

grammar   grammar   _____

If you are **particular (par/tic/u/lar)** that means you are picky.

particular   particular   _____

Peculiar (pe/cu/li/ar) means strange.

peculiar   peculiar   _____

If something is **popular (po/pu/lar)**, then a lot of people like it.

popular   popular   _____

A **regular (reg/u/lar)** drink is small.

regular   regular   _____

If someone asks you a question, you **answer (an/swer)** it.

answer   answer   _____

You should **consider (con/si/der)** other people's feelings.

consider   consider   _____

A **quarter (quar/ter)** can be written as $^1/_4$.

quarter   quarter   _____

Make sure you **remember (re/mem/ber)** your mum's birthday!

remember   remember   _____

Now test yourself without looking at the words and **check for yourself** if you got them all right. Practice writing any words that you made mistakes on again.

The letters ough can be used to represent a number of sounds and a very few words use the letters ear to represent the sound (ir).

Remember: Say the word aloud, then say each letter aloud **as you write it** e.g. 'though, t ... h ... o ... u ... g ... h'

Even **though** these words are tricky to spell, you need to learn them.

though   _though_   _____

Although (al/though) these words are tricky, you need to learn them.

although   _although_   _____

You need to eat **enough (e/nough)** fruit and veg to stay healthy.

enough   _enough_   _____

A **thought** is an idea that you have in your mind.

thought   _thought_   _____

A child can fit **through** a smaller gap than an adult.

through   _through_   _____

If you get ill, you may have a **cough**.

cough   _cough_   _____

You need to get up **early (ear/ly)** enough to get to school on time.

early   _early_   _____

Have you **heard** the news today?

heard   _heard_   _____

Earth is another name for soil.

earth   _earth_   _____

You need to **learn** to spell these words.

learn   _learn_   _____

Now test yourself without looking at the words and <u>**check for yourself**</u> if you got them all right. Practice writing any words that you made mistakes on again.

Very few words use the letters ei or the letters ea to represent the long (a) sound and very few words have a silent u in them, like in the words below.

Remember: Say the word aloud, then say each letter aloud **as you write it** e.g. 'vein, v ... e ... i ... n'

A **vein** takes blood back to your heart.

vein   _vein_   _____

August is the **eighth** month of the year.

eighth   _eighth_   _____

Weight can be measured in kilograms.

weight   _weight_   _____

A **straight** line does not bend or curve.

straight   _straight_   _____

Great means very good.

great   _great_   _____

Steak is a type of meat that comes from a cow.

steak   _steak_   _____

Some people have a cup of tea when they take a **break**.

break   _break_   _____

Have you ever had a toy that you need to **build**?

build   _build_   _____

A **guard** is given the job of protecting someone or something.

guard   _guard_   _____

A tour **guide** will tell you about a place that you visit.

guide   _guide_   _____

Now test yourself without looking at the words and **check for yourself** if you got them all right. Practice writing any words that you made mistakes on again.

The words below are words that mostly stick to the spelling rules that you have already learnt.

Remember: Say the word aloud, then say each letter aloud **as you write it** e.g. 'address, a ... d ... d ... r ... e ... s ... s'

Your **address (ad/dress)** is where you live.

address　　　*address*　_____

Do you normally **arrive (ar/rive)** at school on time?

arrive　　　*arrive*　_____

Boys are **different (dif/fer/ent)** to girls.

different　　　*different*　_____

If something is **difficult (dif/fi/cult)**, it is hard to do.

difficult　　　*difficult*　_____

Scientists can do an **experiment (ex/per/i/ment)** to test an idea.

experiment　　*experiment*　_____

February (Feb/ru/ary) is the second month of the year.

February　　　*February*　_____

In **history (his/tor/y)** you learn about the past.

history　　　*history*　_____

Can you **imagine (i/ma/gine)** being an adult?

imagine　　　*imagine*　_____

It is **important (im/por/tant)** that you always try your best.

important　　*important*　_____

You should show **interest (in/ter/est)** when people talk to you.

interest　　　*interest*　_____

Now test yourself without looking at the words and <u>check for yourself</u> if you got them all right. Practice writing any words that you made mistakes on again.

The words below are words that mostly stick to the spelling rules that you have already learnt.

Remember: Say the word aloud, then say each letter aloud **as you write it** e.g. 'length, l ... e ... n ... g ... t ... h'

What **length** is your hair: short, medium or long?

length   _length_   _____

You can gain more **knowledge (know/ledge)** if you read more books.

knowledge   _knowledge_   _____

If something is **natural (na/tu/ral)**, then it just happens.

natural   _natural_   _____

If you do something **often (of/ten)**, you do it a lot.

often   _often_   _____

Perhaps (per/haps) we should not eat anymore ice-cream.

perhaps   _perhaps_   _____

If something is **possible (pos/si/ble)**, then it can be done.

possible   _possible_   _____

Potatoes (po/ta/toes) are a type of vegetable.

potatoes   _potatoes_   _____

It will **probably (pro/bab/ly)** rain in January.

probably   _probably_   _____

A **sentence (sen/tence)** should start with a capital letter.

sentence   _sentence_   _____

If you **separate (se/pa/rate)** things, you move them away from each other.

separate   _separate_   _____

Now test yourself without looking at the words and **check for yourself** if you got them all right. Practice writing any words that you made mistakes on again.

The sound (ij) is represented by the letters age at the end of words of more than one syllable, like in the words below.

Remember: Say the word aloud, then say each letter aloud **as you write it** e.g. 'bandage, b ... a ... n ... d ... a ... g ... e'

A nurse will tie a **bandage (ban/dage)** around a bad cut.

bandage   *bandage*   _____

English is the main **language (lan/guage)** that people speak in the UK.

language   *language*   _____

A **village (vil/lage)** is smaller than a town.

village   *village*   _____

If you drop something, you can **damage (dam/age)** it.

damage   *damage*   _____

If something is **average (a/ver/age)** it is normal.

average   *average*   _____

Another name for a picture is an **image (im/age)**.

image   *image*   _____

If you **encourage (en/cou/rage)** someone, you help them to keep going.

encourage   *encourage*   _____

You can send a **message (mes/sage)** by email or by text.

message   *message*   _____

A **cottage (cot/tage)** is a small house in the countryside.

cottage   *cottage*   _____

A **garage (gar/age)** is used for parking a car.

garage   *garage*   _____

Now test yourself without looking at the words and **check for yourself** if you got them all right. Practice writing any words that you made mistakes on again.

All of the words below represent at least one sound in an unusual way. Each part of the word that is unusual is underlined to help you to remember it.

Remember: Say the word aloud, then say each letter aloud **as you write it** e.g. 'believe, b ... e ... l ... i ... e ... v ... e'

If you **bel<u>ie</u>ve (be/lieve)** something, then you think that it is true.

believe   believe   _____

You **breath<u>e</u>** air in and out all of the time.

breathe   breathe   _____

A **b<u>u</u>siness (bus/i/ness)** tries to make money.

business   business   _____

To have a **gr<u>ou</u>p** of people, you need to have more than one person.

group   group   _____

A **min<u>u</u>te (min/ute)** is 60 seconds.

minute   minute   _____

The teacher is not happy if the class is **na<u>ugh</u>ty (naugh/ty)**.

naughty   naughty   _____

Your birthday is a special **occasion (oc/ca/sion)**.

occasion   occasion   _____

It is OK to eat sweets **occasionally (oc/ca/sion/al/ly)**.

occasionally   occasionally   _____

Your mum is a **w<u>o</u>man (wo/man)**.

woman   woman   _____

Some **w<u>o</u>men (wo/men)** like to wear dresses.

women   women   _____

Now test yourself without looking at the words and **<u>check for yourself</u>** if you got them all right. Practice writing any words that you made mistakes on again.

All of the words below represent at least one sound in an unusual or tricky way. Each part of the word that is unusual is underlined to help you to remember it.

Remember: Say the word aloud, then say each letter aloud **as you write it** e.g. 'forward, f … o … r … w … a … r … d'

What do you most look **forward (for/ward)** to doing?

forward   forward _____

A **library (li/bra/ry)** has lots of books in it.

library   library _____

If something is **ordinary (or/din/ar/y)**, it is normal.

ordinary   ordinary _____

If you **notice (no/tice)** something, you spot it.

notice   notice _____

Something you have not done before is a new **experience (ex/per/i/ence)**.

experience   experience _____

Plastic is one type of **material (ma/ter/i/al)**.

material   material _____

Purpose (pur/pose) means the reason that you do something.

purpose   purpose _____

Left and right are **opposite (op/po/site)** to each other.

opposite   opposite _____

Your **favourite (fa/vou/rite)** toy is the toy that you like the most.

favourite   favourite _____

Matches are dangerous; **therefore (there/fore)** you should not play with them.

therefore   therefore _____

Now test yourself without looking at the words and **check for yourself** if you got them all right. Practice writing any words that you made mistakes on again.

When you add a vowel suffix to a word of more than one syllable that ends vowel-consonant, if the last syllable is stressed / emphasised, then you need to double the final consonant

Base word + Suffix	New word	1st try	2nd try	3rd try
forgot + en	forgotten	*forgotten*		
upset + ing	upsetting	*upsetting*		
admit + ed	admitted	*admitted*		
begin + er	beginner	*beginner*		
forbid + en	forbidden	*forbidden*		
control + ing	controlling	*controlling*		
equip + ed	equipped	*equipped*		
prefer + ed	preferred	*preferred*		
occur + ing	occurring	*occurring*		

When you add a vowel suffix to a word of more than one syllable that ends vowel-consonant, if the last syllable is NOT stressed / emphasised, then you do NOT double the final consonant

Base word + Suffix	New word	1st try	2nd try	3rd try
garden + ing	gardening	gardening	_____	_____
visit + ed	visited	visited	_____	_____
limit + ing	limiting	limiting	_____	_____
benefit + ed	benefited	benefited	_____	_____
open + ing	opening	opening	_____	_____
gallop + ed	galloped	galloped	_____	_____
target + ing	targeting	targeting	_____	_____
carpet + ed	carpeted	carpeted	_____	_____
magnet + ism	magnetism	magnetism	_____	_____

The prefix inter means between or among.

The prefix super means above or greater than.

Prefix + Base word	New word	1st try	2nd try	3rd try
inter + city	intercity	intercity		
inter + act	interact	interact		
inter + national	international	international		
inter + change	interchange	interchange		
Super + man	Superman	Superman		
super + market	supermarket	supermarket		
super + star	superstar	superstar		
super + store	superstore	superstore		
super + visor	supervisor	supervisor		

The prefix anti means against or not.

The prefix auto means self or own.

Prefix + Base word	New word	1st try	2nd try	3rd try
anti + dote	antidote	antidote		
anti + septic	antiseptic	antiseptic		
anti + clockwise	anticlockwise	anticlockwise		
anti + social	antisocial	antisocial		
anti + biotic	antibiotic	antibiotic		
auto + matic ('matic' is not a base word)	automatic	automatic		
auto + graph	autograph	autograph		
auto + mate	automate	automate		
auto + mobile	automobile	automobile		

Passwords for Year 4 Spelling Games on www.SaveTeachersSundays.com

Password	Spelling games
c3v0n	tion words
x1zwe	ation games
dc4b7	sion games
cno1z	ssion and cian games
db2cr	ous, not as a suffix games
vom29	Suffix ous (change ous to or) games
cvr5n	Suffix ous (drop e and change y to i) games
a8x5z	Suffix ly games (just add) games
evr90	Suffix ly games (drop e) games
cbp1z	Suffix ly games (double l) games
zop9q	Suffix ly games (change y to i) games
qa4vu	Suffix ly games (add ally) games
c30zq	Suffix en games
vp2z0	Suffix ity games
o10xc	Doubling the Final Consonant games
q2c9l	Prefix dis games
apl10	Prefix mis games
awlb2	Prefix in and Prefix un games
id30v	Prefix im games
bin2z	Prefix il and Prefix ir games
verz0	Prefix re and Prefix sub games
abop2	Prefix anti and Prefix auto games
vpz3n	Prefix inter and Prefix super games
oxl2a	(k) as ch 1 games
cqzp3	(k) as ch 2 games
cqp3m	(s) as sc games

Passwords for Year 4 Spelling Games on www.SaveTeachersSundays.com

Password	Spelling games
pola6	–age games
vq2z9	–ar and –er games
vw2g1	–gue and –que games
zpm1c	ic games
zoc1z	Long (a) as ei and ea and Silent u games
apm1c	ough and (ir) as ear games
ol2cu	Short (u) as ou games
xqz2b	y as a vowel (short i) 1 games
bq90m	y as a vowel (short i) 2 games
3v7hu	y as a vowel (short i) 3 games
cqz70	Regular Words 1 games
mqolp	Regular Words 2 games
cqz70	Irregular Words 1 games
1qs4b	Irregular Words 2 games
cw2z0	or games
pqc3b	ore games
yu2z6	oar and our games
xq2z0	aw in the middle of words games
mvop3	aw at the end of words games
oe30c	au games
vnie3	all games
cqz80	(or) homophones games
veb34	wor games
cbpo1	wa, swa and squa games
cqz23	ble and -dle games
ui78b	fle and -gle games

Passwords for Year 4 Spelling Games on www.SaveTeachersSundays.com

Password	Spelling games
yzp09	tle and -kle games
ymq2c	ple, -stle, -cle and -zle games
cw1z6	al games
nb90q	el games
kaop9	ture games
o9jqc	ture and -sure games
b2z0f	kn- games
fl10c	wr- games
bwc93	gn- and -il games
cq2z0	wh- games
nvui9	ph- games
qw3c5	Soft c games
c2zio	ce games
plx4v	se games
be37s	Soft g games
sn89m	ge games
mq4c4	dge games
c2z0p	Short (e) as ea words 1 games
p3lv8	Short (e) as ea words 2 games
nvo40	Short (u) as o words
ver34	Change y to i games
ni6ca	Change y to i and add es games
o10xc	Double the final consonant games

Printed in Poland
by Amazon Fulfillment
Poland Sp. z o.o., Wrocław